W9-ACZ-993

# THE POLITICAL USES OF SEA POWER

*Studies in International Affairs Number 23*

Studies in International Affairs Number 23

# THE POLITICAL USES OF SEA POWER

*by Edward N. Luttwak*

CARL A. RUDISILL LIBRARY
LENOIR RHYNE COLLEGE

*The Washington Center of Foreign Policy Research*
*School of Advanced International Studies*
*The Johns Hopkins University*

*The Johns Hopkins University Press*
*Baltimore and London*

*359.03*

*L97p*

*10 0425*

*Mar. 1977*

Copyright © 1974 by The Johns Hopkins University Press
All rights reserved. No part of this book may be
reproduced or transmitted in any form or by any means,
electronic or mechanical, including photocopying,
recording, xerography, or any information storage and
retrieval system, without permission in writing
from the publisher.
Manufactured in the United States of America

The Johns Hopkins University Press, Baltimore, Maryland 21218
The Johns Hopkins University Press Ltd., London

Library of Congress Catalog Card Number 74–8219
ISBN 0–8018–1658–0 (clothbound edition)
ISBN 0–8018–1659–9 (paperbound edition)

Originally published, 1974
Paperbound edition, 1974

Library of Congress Cataloging in Publication data
will be found on the last printed page of this book.

# FOREWORD

As the Cold War takes new forms and economic and energy issues come to the forefront of international politics, we are inclined to forget that the role of military power persists. Like other relationships among states, military relations take many forms which change with the changing structure and dynamics of international politics. If America's conduct of local crises with the Soviet Union, its maintenance of the military security of allies, or its aid to less developed countries against insurgencies seem less urgent, the strategic military balance nonetheless remains a central element of world politics in the agreements and continuing negotiations of American-Soviet arms control; the changing ratio of nuclear strategic strength between the Super Powers remains an active concern; the politics of negotiating mutual force reductions in Europe suffuses East-West and intrawestern relations; India's demonstration of nuclear power recalls old apprehensions of nuclear proliferation in a new context of multipolar diplomacy; the Soviet massing of armed force on China's northern border casts a menacing, if ambiguous, shadow over détente; and the growing reach of Soviet naval power promises to shape the pattern of competition and influence among a number of states in unpredictable ways.

As always, the psychological and political uses of force short of war are varied and pervasive in the relations of states. Indeed, the increased constraints on the overt use of force—particularly the con-

straints on the developed states—continue to enhance the role of force short of war. But neither
the theory nor operational thinking and planning for
the use of force has kept pace with the developing
modes of military suasion. Our concepts, and even
our definitions, for coping with the multiple political
uses of armed force are cloudy and misleading. We
have not related them comprehensively or precisely
to the richness of actual experience.

In this essay, Edward Luttwak makes an important contribution toward closing the gap between
concepts and definitions, on the one hand, and experience, on the other. He does so by examining the
political uses of that realm of military power which
has been traditionally as well as contemporaneously
the most versatile and extensive instrument of foreign policy in peacetime: sea power. His achieve-
ment thereby contributes to one of the principal objec-
tives of the Washington Center of Foreign Policy
Research: to interpret the elements of continuity
and change in the international environment of U.S.
foreign policy.

ROBERT E. OSGOOD, Dean
School of Advanced
International Studies

# CONTENTS

# ACKNOWLEDGMENT

This book was written with the financial support of the Advanced Research Program of the U.S. Naval War College. I wish to acknowledge with deep gratitude the extracurricular kindness and intellectual stimulation I received from the director of the program, James E. King, and the president of the College, Vice Admiral Stansfield Turner. They, like several others at the College, were kind enough to instruct me in the rudiments of sea power, while exploring with me its political dimensions.

# THE POLITICAL USES OF SEA POWER

*Studies in International Affairs Number 23*

# I. THE THEORY OF SUASION

In having a peacetime political function in addition to their combat capabilities, naval forces are like all other forms of military power, only more so. The familiar attributes of an oceanic navy—inherent mobility, tactical flexibility, and a wide geographic reach—render it peculiarly useful as an instrument of policy even in the absence of hostilities. Land-based forces, whether ground or air, can also be deployed in a manner calculated to encourage friends and coerce enemies, but only within the narrow constraints of insertion feasibility, and with inherently greater risks, since the land nexus can convert any significant deployment into a *political* commitment, with all the rigidities that this implies.

In wartime, the political uses of sea power are naturally relegated to the background in the formulation of naval strategy, which concentrates on combat capabilities, i.e., "sea control" and "projection," to use the current jargon of the U.S. Navy.[1] In the absence of general hostilities, however, a reverse priority applies, and though the prolonged confrontation of the Cold War has retarded the process, the focus of Great Power naval strategy

[1] As defined in the 1972 and 1973 posture statements; e.g., Statement of Admiral Elmo R. Zumwalt, Jr., USN, Chief of Naval Operations, on Department of Defense Appropriations, FY 1973, U.S. Congress, Senate, *Hearings before the Senate Committee on Appropriations,* 92nd Cong., 2d Sess., 1972, Pt. 3-Navy, p. 67.

has been shifting to missions that are "political" in the sense that their workings rely on the reactions of others, and these are reactions that naval deployments may evoke, but cannot directly induce.

In order to evaluate the political impact of naval deployments and assess their political utility, the distinct *modes* in which any political effects are generated must be defined and classified, just as the combat capabilities of a fleet are assessed by computing the different tactical and strategic capabilities that are found within it. Just as such an assessment is based on a previous classification of the various functional missions (anti-submarine, anti-shipping, interdiction on land), a political evaluation requires its own system of analytical classification, even if the precision and stability of any definition in this area must inevitably be limited. A set of definitions has accordingly been presented below to avoid the use of terms that have already acquired unwanted and possibly misleading connotations.[2] These defini-

_____

[2] There is no shortage of such terms. Even "presence" has an unfortunate connotation in that it implies physical visibility where none may exist. More important, it suggests passivity where none may be intended—or perceived. One typical erroneous deduction is that submarines are inherently unsuitable for "presence" missions. In fact, even a ballistic-missile submarine has been used to assert a (strategic-nuclear) "presence." (For example, the SSBN "Patrick Henry" visited Izmir in 1963 to reaffirm the inclusion of Turkey within the scope of strategic-nuclear deterrence following the removal of the land-based IRBMs previously deployed on her soil.) The literature also includes "interposition," valid enough to describe instances of effective blockade but otherwise anachronistic in its associa-

tions are based on the conveniently neutral term "suasion," whose own meaning usefully suggests the indirectness of any political application of naval force.

## ARMED SUASION IN GENERAL

If one tries to disentangle the role of the U.S. Sixth Fleet in a major international event such as the 1972 expulsion/withdrawal of Russian forces from Egypt, one would have to begin by isolating the third-party and adversary reactions which the Sixth Fleet may reasonably be deemed to have evoked. Some are obvious. First, by virtue of its perceived capabilities, by its role as a major asset and symbol of the United States, and through the intermittent manifestation of political will in Washington with respect to its possible use, the Sixth Fleet foreclosed a number of military options otherwise open to the Russian leadership. This represents *latent* suasion in a *deterrent* mode at various levels

---

tions with the age of line-of-sight gunnery. A British battleship could no longer rely on "interposition" to protect (Basque refugee) ships from a modern counterpart to the nationalist cruisers of the Spanish Civil War, if the latter were equipped with maneuverable SSMs—unless that is, "interposition" implies a direct (deterrent) threat which would in fact deprive the concept of its peculiar meaning, and analytical worth. A new classification is presented in James Cable's recent study, *Gunboat Diplomacy: Political applications of limited naval force* (New York: Praeger for The Institute for Strategic Studies, 1970). His definitions, "definitive," "purposeful," "catalytic," and "expressive" force, intermingle functional and intensity criteria. As a result they are more useful for descriptive than for analytical purposes.

3

of intensity. These Russian options obviously included a range of offensive moves with respect to Israel, and the Sixth Fleet thus precluded Russian actions that could have enhanced the alliance-worth of the Soviet Union in Egyptian eyes. This in itself can be deemed to have been one of the basic causes of the event to be explained.

A second effect was also latent but *supportive* rather than deterrent: Turkey, a vulnerable ally in control of the Straits, was given tacit support by the presence of the Sixth Fleet. This tended to strengthen Turkish resolve to continue to enforce the Montreux Convention rules which affect Russian use of the Straits; and of course these rules would prejudice the security of any Russian naval, or sea-supported, forces on the far side of the Straits in the event of war.

A third effect, also latent and supportive, was felt by the Israelis. While the Sixth Fleet strengthened Israeli resolve to resist Russian pressures and threats (by providing an "insurance" element in their calculations), its presence also militated against Israeli activism, since the net incentive of a pre-emptive attack on the Russian forces in the area was much reduced by the ultimate security that the Sixth Fleet was thought to offer. As a result, the Fleet was instrumental both in encouraging Israeli resistance to the Russians (which devalued the worth of the Russian connection to Egypt), and in preventing a very dangerous Israeli move, a move that could not have been excluded from the realm

4

of possibility given the open-ended and ominous nature of the Russian build-up in Egypt in 1970.

A fourth, one-time effect, manifest at an earlier point in time, was an example of *active* suasion, both *coercive* and *supportive:* the declaratory intervention of the United States in the 1970 Syrian-Jordanian crisis. In this instance, there was both a negative (i.e., deterrent) mode of coercion, in that the United States sought to prevent a Russian intervention, and a positive ("compellent") mode, in that the United States demanded that Syria withdraw its armor from Jordan, for which the Palestinian cover was too thin to be plausible. The supportive element of this instance of active suasion was of secondary importance, because reports indicate that the Jordanian leadership was already fully resolved to resist the Syrian attack; nevertheless, the insurance provided by the "projection" capabilities of the Sixth Fleet must have intruded on Jordanian calculations by reducing any incentive to seek a political settlement and a fresh compromise with the Palestinian military organizations. What makes this one-time application of sea power *active* is the nature of the operation: it involved specific, though not necessarily overt, American demands. The fact that the operation also involved redeployment and reinforcement of the Sixth Fleet is not, on the other hand, fundamental to our distinction between *latent* and *active* suasion.

Whether it is active or latent, coercive or supportive, deterrent or positive (i.e., "compellent"),

5

*armed suasion* is manifest only in others' reactions; it is the general concept that embraces all such reactive effects. Any instrument of military power that can be used to inflict damage upon an adversary, physically limit his freedom of action, or reveal his intentions [3] may also affect his conduct, and that of any interested third parties, even if force is never actually used. The necessary (but by no means sufficient) condition is that the parties concerned *perceive* (correctly or otherwise) the capabilities deployed, thus allowing these capabilities to intrude on their view of the policy environment and so affect their decisions. Armed suasion, therefore, applies to others' reactions, and not the actions, or the intent, of the deploying party. The latter may exercise suasion in order to evoke certain reactions, but cannot achieve them directly, as combat effects can be achieved by the application of force.

Because suasion can only operate through the filters of others' perceptions, the exercise of suasion is inherently unpredictable in its results. Routine fleet movements which were not intended to pose a threat may be seen by others as threatening (since the threat is *latent* in the forces themselves). On the other hand, a deliberate but tacit threat may be ignored, or worse, may evoke contrary reactions. In addition, in the decision-making arena of the target state, the threat (or supportive) perceptions evoked by the forces deployed have to compete with all

[3] Vice Admiral Stansfield Turner, President (1974) of the U.S. Naval War College, suggested this point in conversation.

6

TABLE I. THE POLITICAL APPLICATION OF NAVAL POWER: A TYPOLOGY

**Armed Suasion in General**
*(all types; all modes; all levels of intensity)*

**Naval Suasion**
*(specific to sea-based/sea-related forces)*

**Latent Naval Suasion**
*(reactions evoked by routine and/or undirected deployments)*

- Supportive Mode
- Deterrent Mode

**Active Naval Suasion**
*(reactions evoked by any deliberate action or signal)*

- Supportive
  *(reaction: the target—ally/client—is reassured)*
- Coercive
  - Positive *(i.e., "compellence")*
  - Negative *(i.e., deterrence)*

other political pressures that have a bearing on the decision, and the final outcome of this complex interaction is impossible to predict.

The exercise of armed suasion in peacetime need not exclude the actual use of force, where the use is "symbolic." Because this is the era of undeclared conflicts brought about by the new and significant inhibitions to the overt initiation of war that have become manifest since 1945—the term "peacetime" now defines only the absence of *general* hostilities conducted at a *high* level of intensity. It follows that no firm dividing line can be established between the use of threats and the actual infliction of damage albeit in small doses. As long as the purpose and context of the use of force remains political, i.e., intended to evoke suasion effects rather than to destroy enemy forces or values, it cannot be arbitrarily excluded from the range of political instrumentalities provided by naval forces in "peacetime." But the political use of symbolic forces *does* require that the target state recognize its symbolic nature, i.e., that the damage inflicted has been *deliberately* minimized. This in turn requires the deploying state to discriminate successfully between what is and what is not symbolic in terms of others' perceptions, which may be quite different from its own. The same bombing raid by ten F-4s may be seen in Cairo as the beginning of a large-scale attack; in Washington and Hanoi, as purely symbolic; and in, say, Damascus as an all-out air offensive. In other words, the use of symbolic force as a way of augmenting coercive suasion entails an additional element of uncertainty.

Nor is the exercise of suasion predicated on the absence of hostilities, even general hostilities. During World War I, *tactical* suasion kept the High Seas Fleet well clear of Atlantic shipping lanes; it also kept units of the Grand Fleet from bombarding U-boat bases on the Flemish coast. The former case of tactical suasion was based on German *perceptions* of British naval power that may or may not have included a full appreciation of the vulnerability of the Grand Fleet, including its defective large-calibre shells and the weak horizontal armor of its battle-cruisers. Similarly, the deterrence evoked by western anti-submarine warfare forces may continue to operate on the Russian submarine force, even if the increasingly unlikely prospect of a Russian offensive in western Europe were to materialize. In the past, such deterrence may have tacitly discouraged the Russians from exercising the option of a submarine campaign against western shipping, and such deterrence would not cease merely because of the outbreak of hostilities. If peace is divisible, so is deterrence.

Because armed suasion operates on both the tactical and the political level, contradictions between the two may occur, thus presenting very serious decision-making problems. One may readily visualize a situation in which the tactical suasion of, say, greatly reinforced Russian naval and naval-air forces based in Egypt and Syria could discourage

the U.S. Navy from deploying its own forces in the
eastern Mediterranean for reasons of elementary
military prudence, while at the same time at the
political level it may be thought that the worth of
continued deployment was greater than ever. Political considerations would normally be of overriding importance in the decision-making arena, but
only if the issue reaches the political level. If all
concerned, on all sides, share the same perception
of the balance of forces, the problem should not
arise, since unviable forces would be discounted as
either threats or supporting elements in the power
equation (except in extreme cases where military
forces are made hostages to commitments). More
commonly, however, the same set of rival forces is
evaluated quite differently in different quarters so
that given our hypothetical Russian build-up, for
example, the Sixth Fleet could at the same time be
very vulnerable and yet still seen as very useful in
the political arena. Since men at the tactical and
political levels have quite different responsibilities,
contradictions between the two levels of suasion
can be a source of acute internal controversy, just
as the conflict between tactical and political priorities
has been a chronic source of tension between soldiers
and politicians in times of war.

   To summarize, "armed suasion" defines all reactions, political or tactical, elicited by all parties—
allies, adversaries, or neutrals—to the existence,
display, manipulation, or symbolic use of any instrument of military power, whether or not such

reactions reflect any deliberate intent of the deploying party. "Naval suasion" refers to effects evoked
by sea-based or sea-related forces.

## Latent Suasion

Effects evoked by the deliberate exercise of armed
suasion where the intention is to elicit a given reaction from a specified party are defined as "active"
in what follows. As against this, the undirected, and
hence possibly unintended, reactions evoked by
naval deployments maintained on a routine basis are
defined as "latent." Latent naval suasion continuously shapes the military dimension of the total
environment which policy-makers perceive and
within which they operate. By those who perceive
them, the specific capabilities deployed are seen as
potential threats or potential sources of support.
As such, they influence the behavior of those who
deem themselves to be within reach of the forces
concerned.

In the deterrent mode, the range of capabilities
perceived sets a series of tacit limits on the actions
that may otherwise have been considered desirable
or, at any rate, feasible. In this sense, one should
not speak of a "presence" so much as of a shadow
that impinges on the freedom of action of adversaries, because the capabilities perceived can be
activated at any time, while the formulation of the
intent to use them can be both silent and immediate.
The ultimate readiness to resort to force is, of
course, indispensable; without it there can be no

armed suasion whether latent or of any other type.[4]
It is therefore misleading to make any dichotomy
between "peacetime presence" and "wartime" combat capabilities, since a "presence" can have no
significant effect in the absence of *any* possibility
that the transition to war will be made. Latent suasion is therefore the most general (in terms of intensity) and geographically the most widespread
form of deterrence; as such, it is likely to be the
most important class of benefits generated by sea
power. More will be said about deterrence as such
below. Here it is only necessary to note the inherently tacit nature of latent deterrence and its
major implications: first, the wide scope for mis-
calculation that the tacit nature of this form of
deterrence inevitably implies; second, the greater

[4] This "resolve" to use force is not a generalized psychological propensity but rather the reflection of a given policy
priority. This priority in turn must derive from an assessment
of the importance of the object of a confrontation. The *credibility* of a party in the eyes of others, i.e., his resolve, will
depend on others' estimates of how he views the interests in
dispute. One cannot, therefore, hope to "show resolve" or
augment one's credibility in a confrontation by the artful
manipulation of images and the use of signals conveyed by
means of symbolic force independently of the importance of the
*object* of a confrontation. There is, of course, some scope for
the diplomatic manipulation of others' policy images so as to
magnify one's interests in others' eyes, but the rationality nexus
cannot be cut entirely. Thus, the defense of Berlin can be
assimilated to the survival of the United States by prolonged
and successful diplomatic image-making and the odd dramatic
gesture (Kennedy's "I am a Berliner"), but few localities in
dispute can be turned into a Berlin which strategic-nuclear
forces alone suffice to protect.

12

flexibility of this form of deterrence, in that in the event of a failure there is no compulsion to carry out an act of retaliation that was never threatened overtly; third, the corresponding weakening of deterrence where no rigid commitment to implement retaliation obtains. To speak softly while carrying a big stick may be less effective as a deterrent than to make a firm, overt commitment to use a rather smaller stick.

The second mode of latent suasion is supportive. The deployment of naval forces is a continuous reminder to allies and clients of the capabilities that can be brought to their aid. Moreover, with its ready intervention potential, a fleet can give a tangible content to any prior commitments that may have been made. Normally, the effects of this mode of suasion are seen as solely beneficial: allies are encouraged to adhere to alliance policies and dissuaded from conciliating adversaries at the expense of the senior ally. But because the support thus given can broaden the range of options open to allies and clients, the net effects of this mode of suasion can also be negative. For example, while the U.S. Sixth Fleet may be continuously deterring Russian and Arab moves against American interests as well as reinforcing the Alliance, it may also be giving unintended encouragement to Israeli activism in a manner inimical to the interests of the United States.

Given its inherent indirection, the latent suasion of naval forces can therefore produce undesirable side-effects, from the deploying party's point of view. Ground and air forces can also do so, but in their case the latent effects they generate will be as static and geographically limited as the forces themselves. Naval forces, however, because of their unimpeded mobility, entail the possibility of diffused and unrecognized latent effects, including undesirable ones. By the same token, however, once the undesirable effects are recognized, adjustments can be made quickly and silently. If, for example, a routine fleet movement off the coast of India is thought capable of evoking undesirable reactions from the Indian government, the transit route can be shifted to the south, and with none of the rigidities, either technical or political, associated with the redeployment of land-based forces. Thus, the same quality of sea power that is the source of possible political difficulties can also provide, through its inherent flexibility, the means to avoid them, if, that is, any negative political repercussions are in fact perceived. This suggests that continuous political guidance of the highest possible quality is a crucial requirement of overseas naval deployments: a modern oceanic fleet needs a political "radar" as much as it needs the electronic variety.

Even if high-grade political advisers are active in naval commands, and even if they are acute observers of the political "radiation" emitted by the fleet, the problem cannot be fully solved since there may be, and often are, severe distortions in others' perceptions of the fleet—of its tactical configuration and the underlying political intent of its movements.

Generally, political leaders around the world understand more about ground power than air power, and more about the latter than about naval power. In the case of active suasion, decision-makers on the other side will at least be faced with a definite grouping of capabilities in the naval forces that are displayed to them, or positioned against them, and the intent of the deploying party will normally be conveyed to them in one form or another. But in the case of latent suasion, neither of these conditions obtains; the political leaders of the littoral states must therefore construe the capabilities and intent of the naval forces which they observe according to their wits, and the possibilities of distortion are vast. For one thing, leaders of the smaller littoral states have ready access to naval expertise only in their own small navies, whose officers may know little about the operation of Great Power navies. With respect to political questions, one national leader is as good as another since each must make his own judgments in the light of his own world-view. But assessments of naval capabilities, of the significance of particular tactical configurations, and of the nature of the possible threats emanating from the sea require technical knowledge that many smaller states do not have.

Even those, like the Israelis, who have shown some competence in the conduct and analysis of land and air warfare may have no such expertise

15

with respect to naval matters. There is no land or air counterpart to the naval errors made by the Israelis: the imprudent conduct of the "Elath," the loss of the "Dakar," the explosion of ill-loaded landing craft in harbor and others.[5] Moreover, in the many backward countries where military men have seized power, very few sailors seem to have reached positions of political significance, barring the odd Turkish admiral. How do these leaders assess the relative capabilities of the American and Russian fleets? How do they evaluate the balance of sea power in their region of the world? Do they count ships and ship-classes by referring to *Jane's*? Do they use aggregate tonnage figures, once elevated to the dignity of a treaty standard, but now so obviously misleading in the presence of rapid technological change? These and related problems will be discussed in Chapter II. In this context, it suffices to say that the relationship between the forces deployed and the suasion effects that these forces actually evoke is neither direct nor proportional.

Since latent suasion is undirected and not overtly linked to any specific policy objective, its net ef-

[5] In the 1956 Sinai Campaign a key objective, Rafah, was to be attacked on land in the wake of naval bombardment by a French destroyer. The Israeli command assumed that the bombardment would annihilate the Egyptian defenses even though a single destroyer (three twin five-inch guns) was involved. One hundred and fifty shells were fired, and with little effect. In his *Diary of the Sinai Campaign* (London: Weidenfeld and Nicolson, 1967), p. 74, Moshe Dayan candidly admitted that his expectation had been based on memories of the war films that he had seen, and little else.

fects, and even more, its net benefits, are difficult to identify and impossible to measure. This would not have disturbed Athenians or nineteenth-century Britons, but given the prevailing tendency to attempt the quantification of the benefits generated by military deployments, the elusive nature of latent suasion is something of a policy problem in itself. In this study, particular attention will therefore be given to the identification and evaluation of the deterrent and supportive effects of latent suasion on adversaries, allies, and third parties.

## ACTIVE SUASION

Any system of definitions imposed on the fluid and variegated realm of politics will inevitably be both arbitrary and incomplete. But a typology such as the one presented here is only meant to be convenient for analytical purposes: one need not distort every marginal phenomenon in order to obtain a "good fit." With this thought in mind, the *exercise* of "active" suasion is defined as any deliberate attempt to evoke a specific reaction on the part of others, whether allies, enemies, or neutrals; the reaction actually obtained would constitute the suasion process itself, in this case labeled as active. For example, an attempt to deter an attacker by deploying retaliatory forces and issuing appropriate warnings would constitute the *exercise* of active suasion, while any deterrence in fact achieved would define the suasion effect itself. This to emphasize yet again that we are dealing here with others' reactions, and

17

not with any objective that can be achieved by the direct application of force in itself.

A very important and much studied form of active suasion, all of it armed but so far only partly naval, is the strategic-nuclear level of deterrence. All forms of deterrence, from that which ensures good manners when foreign warships meet at sea, to that which is intended to avert the lethal threat of strategic-nuclear attack by posing an equally lethal retaliatory threat, are based on the same set of interactions, in which psychological elements are of critical importance: first, the deploying party's prior perception of a threat; second, the development and continuous maintenance of strike-back forces capable, even after absorbing an attack, of inflicting damage deemed to be unacceptable by the other party; third, the target party's recognition of the causal link between the retaliatory threat and the specific actions of his that the deploying party is seeking to avert; and, fourth, the target party's concurrence with the value judgments and technical assessments made by the deploying party. *Both* must believe that the retaliatory threat is capable of destroying *greater* values than those which the target party can obtain by making the move that is to be deterred.

In the strategic-nuclear arena, these requirements of deterrence have been the subject of so much scrutiny and debate that their reiteration is unnecessary. But this is not so in respect of lower-intensity levels of deterrence: substrategic forms of deterrence are all too often seen in narrow technical terms. While due attention is given to the mechanics of deterrent deployments, the very demanding psychological requirements of deterrence tend to be discounted. *And it is precisely in respect of the latter that deterrence is apt to fail.* If, to quote Mr. Cable,[6] the Israeli destroyer "Elath" was patrolling the coasts of Sinai in 1967 with an "imprudence scarcely rivalled since the ill-fated patrol of the Broad Fourteens by H.M. ships *Aboukir, Cressy and Hogue,*" this was so because the Israelis were convinced that a deterrent was at work to protect their otherwise very vulnerable destroyer. They must have known that "Styx"-launching patrol boats were in the vicinity; that the "Elath" was sailing well within range of those boats as it turned back off Port Said; and, that the "Elath" was entirely incapable of intercepting or deflecting anti-ship missiles. But the Israelis tacitly assumed that their own ability to shell the cities and industries in the Canal area rendered their own destroyer immune from attack, as in the case of most other Israeli maritime assets, whose protection has always been ensured by deterrence and not by defense.

All the physical requirements of deterrence were fulfilled, because Israeli artillery was in place and within range. The relative-value requirement was also fulfilled, because whatever the scale of values held by the Egyptian leaders, it was obvious that they could hardly judge the worth of an old Z-class destroyer (symbolism included) as greater than that

[6] Cable, *Gunboat Diplomacy,* p. 76.

19

of the vast Egyptian assets that were hostage to Israeli guns. But the third requirement, recognition of the deterrent linkage, was not fulfilled, and the Egyptians proceeded to sink the ship, only to be surprised by the Israeli shelling of Suez that followed.[7]

Since this was an instance of faulty communication that could have been put right by appropriate diplomatic "signaling" before the event, it is not as instructive as another failure of deterrence that occurred between the same antagonists. Following the sinking of the "Elath" on October 21, 1967, there was almost a year of relative quiet on the cease-fire line along the Canal. The small Israeli troop contingents built no "hard" fortifications; shallow earthworks were deemed sufficient since the line was to be held but not defended against major attacks. More than 900,000 Egyptians lived in the Port Said, Ismailiya, and Suez governorates, the most modern and industrialized of all Egyptian provinces.

To the Israelis it seemed apparent that no conceivable tactical hopes could possibly induce the Egyptians to sacrifice their cities and industries by making the Canal the scene of large-scale fighting.[8] A static offensive by fire was in fact the only

[7] It was the contemporary assessment of the Israelis that the Egyptians had been surprised by the *nature* (and intensity) of their response. Comments in the Egyptian press at the time support this deduction. See Muhamad Hasanain Haykal in *Al Ahram,* October 23 and 24, 1967.

[8] See Edward N. Luttwak and Dan Horowitz, *A Study of*

option open to the Egyptian leadership, since it was obvious that a Canal-crossing offensive could not be sustained in the presence of Israel's unchallenged control of the air. Nevertheless, the Israelis discounted the probability of an artillery offensive since, according to *their own scale of values,* its limited, almost symbolic, gains would be outweighed by the destruction of the three governorates' cities and industry. But the Egyptians failed to concur in the relative-value judgment made by the Israelis (condition number 4 of deterrence). In October 1968 the Israeli attempt at protection-by-deterrence collapsed when the Egyptians laid down a series of artillery barrages, and sacrificed the Canal-side cities in order to do so. After this bout of shelling, the Israelis were forced to *defend* the area and to undertake the large-scale construction of "hard" fortifications—at greater cost than would have been the case earlier.

The ultimate source of this error of judgment was the neglect of the significance of cultural differences, and of the differences in relative-value judgments that they imply. Even if it proves to be true that in the strategic-nuclear arena the import of cultural differences is nullified by the world-destroying power of thermonuclear warheads—as all must hope under current offense-only strategic postures—this is certainly not true at lower levels of deterrence. For this reason, and because naval deployments must defend as well as deter in each (substrategic) in-

---

the *Israeli Army* (New York: Harper & Row, forthcoming), for a narrative of this episode.

stance, the body of ideas that has evolved around the theme of strategic-nuclear deterrence is not always a reliable guide to the problems of its somewhat less lethal naval counterparts. For one thing, as it has been suggested, explicit attention must be given to asymmetries in relative-value judgments: the value that our retaliation threatens may seem greater to *us* than the benefit an enemy can obtain by making the attack we seek to deter, but the other side may disagree. This is particularly important in areas such as the Mediterranean region, where two variants of one civilization face an Arab-Islamic culture which is not only very different but which is also undergoing a process of disintegration under the pressure of economic change and nationalism.

This is not the place to discuss the fundamental difference between western patriotism and western nationalism as adopted, and adapted, by Third World nationalists. What is highly relevant, however, is the direct implication that this difference between patriotism and nationalism has for a navy that, among its other goals, is seeking to deter. In essence, this boils down to the observed and amply documented fact that for the convinced nationalist, and hence for those who cater to his values as many Third World regimes do, the tangible values of life and property are less important than such intangibles as a valiant self-image and national (for the leader, personal) honor and glory. As many Europeans did until quite recently (and may do again), convinced nationalists discount the material for the sake of the immaterial, and the latter often comes in the shape of activist policy goals. Once such goals are declared and duly publicized, they commonly acquire an import that is far greater than the commitments made in the more sober context of western policy-formation. Moreover, the highly personalized conduct of policy in many Third World countries implies the absence, or at least weakness, of internal institutional restraints such as those which limit the scope of policies elsewhere. Considering recent American experience in such matters, it would hardly do to claim that there is a *qualitative* difference, but a very significant difference of degree is certainly apparent. The topic will be pursued further in Chapter III; here it suffices to underline the cautionary lessons that apply to the conduct of naval deterrence at the substrategic level: first, the requirement of an explicit (but not, of course, public) linkage between the value to be protected and a retaliatory threat; and, second, the desirability of a maximum "value-spread" between the worth of what is to be protected and the adversary values which are threatened in order to deter. This provides insurance against the effect of poorly understood, and always unpredictable, cultural differences.

A second aspect of naval, substrategic deterrence is the duality of mission requirements: if deterrence fails, defense must take its place. In the event of a failure of deterrence, surviving naval forces are not only expected to conduct retaliatory attacks (which may not be launched at all), but also to remain available for subsequent tasks. Instead of the fixed-intensity retaliation that exhausts the mission of strategic-nuclear forces, naval deterrent forces are expected to retain their tactical flexibility. *And this can be applied to the strengthening or even restoration of deterrence, as well as to defense.* It is for this reason that the symbolic use of force must be retained in the arsenal of political rather than war-fighting instrumentalities. If, for example, preclusive control over a given sea area is asserted by threatening to sink any intruding ships, such deterrence can be reinforced by the deliberate display of the forces deployed for the purpose; should this show signs of failing, deterrence can be rendered yet more intense by demonstrating destructive capabilities, e.g., by shooting "over the bows" of any intruders. Finally, deterrence can be salvaged even after a failure by sinking a single ship, in order to deter the intrusion of the rest, and then by sinking a second and a third and so on, until the line is crossed and the objective becomes destruction rather than suasion in any form. Though "limited exchange scenarios," which envisaged the use of thermonuclear detonations for "signalling" purposes, gained some currency in the strategic debates of the 1960s, such ideas are now recognized as mere fanciful speculation. A similar flexibility is, however, a legitimate and useful attribute of (nonnuclear) naval power applied to the exercise of deterrence.

Though much has been made of the difference between "compellence" and "deterrence," they are generally analogous. Both belong to the realm of coercive suasion, a term that underscores the use of the direct threat, and which suggests an affinity with coercive diplomacy.[9]

Both modes of coercive suasion—the negative, or deterrence, and the positive, or compellence—are subject to the same technical and perceptive requirements; both may be tacit or overt; both may be associated with either private or public warnings; and both are subject to the same psycho-political uncertainties. Since the term was first coined by the banks of the Charles, something of a literature has grown around the concept of "compellence."[10] Its import boils down to the assertion that it is more difficult to compel than to deter since (1) moves are more difficult to reverse than prevent in that the moves to be stopped or reversed may have acquired their own "tactical" and political momentum and (2) public compliance with others' demands would entail additional losses in the way of prestige.

The first purported difference is in fact trivial because, from the point of view of the *offending* party, the factors that lead to a decision to act may be just as forceful as those that may subsequently be

[9] In fact, the two concepts relate to different aspects of the same political phenomenon; each covers one half of a whole that is separated only by institutional boundaries.

[10] The term "compellence" was first used in this sense by Thomas C. Schelling in his *Strategy of Conflict* (Cambridge, Mass.): Harvard University Press, 1960). The term has since acquired general currency.

25

brought to bear against a reversal.[11] Tactical momentum may indeed occur in many cases, but *political* momentum is largely conditioned by whether the second difference obtains or not. And it is with respect to the latter that the distinction between deterrence and compellence as *forms* of coercion seems least warranted, since even if compellence requires actual backtracking rather than the halting of an ongoing activity, it is by no means inevitable that it be made public or be publicly acknowledged. In the case of the Cuba missile crisis, for example, the Russian leadership was able to withhold any admission of compliance from the Soviet media— and this in the context of the most overt and public exercise of compellence imaginable. More typical is the case of Indochina where forces may be advanced or withdrawn by an adversary without any overt recognition, public announcement, or indeed the admission that any forces had moved beyond national borders in the first place. *It is apparent that overt, publicly announced deterrence may be more difficult for the target party to comply with than covert compellence, complied with covertly.*

If it is accepted that both deterrence and compellence are modes of the same coercive form of sua-

---

[11] This can be taken further. Where national leaders have to contend with a "street" opinion that is both activist and ill-informed, the only way of dealing with activist pressures may be to act, and then use others' threats—or actions—as evidence that it is the force of circumstances, and not personal corruption or cowardice, that prevents a more active policy on the part of the national leader.

sion, it follows that the rules of (substrategic) deterrence apply to both. Aside from those discussed on p. 18, one more rule, or rather the qualification of the second rule, should be mentioned at this point: the survivability of the retaliatory forces must be ensured, but not necessarily in the case of enemy attacks that would entail a much higher, qualitatively different level of conflict intensity. While the strike-back requirement is self-explanatory, the qualification appended here derives from a peculiarity of the age: five [12] nations deploy nuclear weapons, but their use is increasingly deemed, by them, to be unacceptable in all situations other than those which entail a threat to national survival. As a result, these weapons can be excluded from the force-level comparisons made in the context of less-than-vital confrontations, even in a direct and central crisis situation. Thus in order to implement the Cuba quarantine of October 1962, the U.S. Navy did require a clear preponderance over Russian naval forces in the area, but it could also be assumed that American warships need not defend against nuclear weapons whether deployed *in situ* or anywhere else. Had the crisis resulted in nuclear war, the ships, or some of them, could have been the target of nuclear attacks, but until that point, nuclear weapons of any sort had no direct effect on the *naval* dimension of the confrontation.

While the fine gradations imagined in the "escala-

[12] Indian plutonium fission devices are not to be counted as weapons—or so the Indian government says.

tion" scenarios of the past with their complex hierarchy of "thresholds" never did have much validity,[13] it is apparent that in any low-intensity naval confrontation nuclear weapons embodied in the forces deployed on either side will not normally play a significant role in assessments of the *local* balance of military strength which, together with the balance of perceived *interests* on either side, will generally determine the outcome of the confrontation. And this will remain so as the intensity of the confrontation increases, until the level is reached where *core* interests come into question.[14] Certainly, as between the Super Powers, it is only when either or both sees the interests in dispute as reaching the life-or-death level that the strategic-nuclear balance enters into play, and does so decisively.[15] Of this the Berlin crises of the late 1950s and early 1960s are the best examples: the West prevailed, though much inferior in terms of local forces, and though not superior in *perceived* strategic-nuclear terms,

[13] Since they ignored the effect of perceptual differences between the two sides, among other things. Here it has been argued that across cultural barriers men may see elephants where there are only mice and vice versa, while the "threshold" concept assumed that men would respond to obscure differences between different breeds of mice—or elephants.

[14] And then the determining factor will be the perceived *strategic*-nuclear balance—as well as the balance of perceived interests.

[15] For a brief discussion of the issue, see Edward N. Luttwak, *The Strategic Balance 1972* (New York: The Library Press for The Center for Strategic and International Studies, Georgetown University, 1972), pp. 69–92.

because the equation successfully made between the survival of Americans at home and the political freedom of Berlin injected strategic-nuclear power into the confrontation, thus nullifying the significance of the *local* (nonnuclear) superiority of the Soviet Union.

Also performed continuously in a latent form, the active variety of *supportive* suasion is exemplified by the visit of the U.S. battleship "Missouri" to Istanbul in March 1946, which inaugurated the postwar deployment of American naval power in the Mediterranean. This spectacular example of naval symbolism represented an attempt to exercise *active* suasion in a *supportive* mode on the Turkish government, then under severe Russian diplomatic pressure.

The "Missouri" episode raises one of the fundamental problems of the political application of naval power: the use of ships as symbols, rather than instruments, of power. There is, in effect, a potential contradiction between the well-understood importance of genuine military superiorities *in situ* in determining the outcome of confrontations and the accepted significance of the symbolic warship. How can the symbolic ship that asserts no local military superiority, and whose capabilities may not even be relevant to the setting, secure the interests of the deploying party? What does the ship-as-symbol really symbolize in fact?

Prevailing views on this score are heavily influenced by a received interpretation of the history of British naval supremacy in the nineteenth and

early twentieth centuries. This is an interpretation
that explains the use of symbolic ships, and much
else, purely in terms of naval power: so long as the
Royal Navy had a globally superior fleet in the
North Sea or anywhere else, a single frigate could
effectively impose the will of H.M. Government
on recalcitrant coastal states the world over, since
the flag it flew was the portent of potentially overwhelming *naval* force. And this was force that
could always be brought to bear if the symbolic
frigate was denied its due. According to this view,
therefore, the symbolic ship derived its powers
from the combat capabilities of the Royal Navy's
battle fleet, and its symbolic power was proportional
to genuine naval power. This conventional interpretation of the British experience of naval supremacy
has now been challenged in a most authoritative
manner by Gerald S. Graham in his lectures on the
"Politics of Naval Supremacy." [16]

Graham's argument is that Great Britain's freedom of action overseas was derived from the paraly-
sis of her European rivals. By virtue of a most successful *continental* policy, the British contrived to
neutralize those powers, especially France, which
could otherwise have competed with Britain overseas. As a result, the targets of British naval pressures were cut off from all aid on the part of
Britain's rivals in Europe, and it was this insulation,
achieved by political means, that forced coastal

[16] Gerald S. Graham, *The Politics of Naval Supremacy*
(Cambridge: Cambridge University Press, 1967).

30

powers overseas to acquiesce in British demands made by a symbolic frigate. Where no such insulation obtained, as in the case of Mehemet Ali's Egypt in the 1830's, the British were in fact unable to enforce compliance with their demands by such means. This implies that the symbolic ship symbolizes *national* rather than *naval* power as such; its effectiveness is thus proportional to the former, not to the latter. Naval power is of course a constituent of national power but it need not be the *salient* source of national power, and hence will not define its limits. Nor will it define the power embodied in the symbolic ship. A navally inferior imperial Germany could project her national power by means of a symbolic warship at Agadir; on the other hand, the continuing supremacy of the Royal Navy after the 1870s did not suffice to prevent a decline in Britain's national power, and thus in the impact of her symbolic ships.

Retrospective assessments of the "Missouri" episode, its perceived significance, and its net effects are consistent with this interpretation of the role of the symbolic ship. For all the majesty of her sixteen-inch guns, her enormous bulk, and uniquely strong armor, the specific tactical capabilities of the "Missouri," or indeed naval capabilities of any kind, were of doubtful relevance to the Russo-Turkish crisis in concrete military terms. The Russian threat to Turkey emanated from the large Russian ground forces and from the associated tactical air power that Stalin could deploy on the Turkish-Bulgarian and Russo-Turkish borders. This was the implied threat behind Russian demands for a renegotiation of the Montreux Convention, and once Turkey recognized that its secular protectors, the British, were no longer up to the task, American support was sought. It is obvious that naval forces could not be injected into this confrontation in a manner that could have altered an exceedingly unbalanced relation of forces between the two sides, since even carrier-based aviation could only have been effective on one half of one sector (the Mediterranean coast of Thrace). But this hardly mattered: the arrival on the scene of the "Missouri" bearing the body of the deceased Turkish ambassador to Washington, was not intended to alter the local balance of power but to affirm a *commitment*. The "Missouri" was an American warship and its journey was a splendid diplomatic gesture that enabled President Truman to make a commitment without "benefit of Congress." [17]

Less sophisticated observers than the Turks or the Russians may have been impressed by the sheer size and formidable guns of the "Missouri," but in this case the warship symbolized presidential willingness to take over the traditional British role in protecting the *Straits'* status quo, and this sufficed to establish an American commitment as far as the

[17] Ferenc A. Váli, *The Turkish Straits and NATO* (Stanford, Calif.: Hoover Institution, 1972), pp. 58–81: and Feridun Cemal Erkin, *Les Rélations Turco-Soviétiques et la question des détroits* (Ankara: 1968), pp. 286–373.

Turks were concerned. (Until then Turkish-American relations had been poor, the main subject of diplomatic communications having been the insistent and futile wartime demands made on the Turks to suspend mineral ore shipments to the Germans. After the "Missouri" episode, however, the Turks felt free to reject Russian demands, acting on the assumption that they had found a new protector in the West.)

We do not know what (coercive/deterrent) impression the "Missouri's" visit made on Stalin's government, but we do know that Russian diplomatic and propaganda pressure on Ankara continued and went on doing so even after the task force built around the carrier "FDR" arrived on the scene, six months after the journey of the "Missouri." On the other hand, by the end of 1946, before the formal enunciation of the Truman Doctrine and its Congressional endorsement, the Russian political offensive against Turkey petered out.

All this suggests that the symbolic warship can play its role only before, and in order to prevent, a confrontation. Its effect on the *local* balance of power may be insignificant, but its purpose is to affirm a commitment of national power, local and strategic, naval or otherwise. In this instance, the symbolic warship was used to affirm a commitment promptly and tangibly in circumstances when political conditions in the United States were such that President Truman was not inclined to seek Congressional approval for a formal commitment by treaty of alliance or unilateral declaration.

If such commitment-making fails to avert a confrontation by its coercive/deterrent suasion effect, then the contest would undergo a change, and only genuine local superiorities would matter in determining the outcome (subject to the rule-setting implications of the strategic balance). It is apparent that nonexistent commitments cannot be simulated by the skillful manipulation of symbolic warships or artful diplomatic imagemaking. Had the Russians felt in 1946 that the maintenance of the status quo in Turkey and the Straits was not considered an important American national interest by the White House, and prospectively, on Capitol Hill, the "Missouri" visit could have had no impact on their own decisions with respect to Turkey. (Perhaps this is what they *did* believe, since Russian pressure on Turkey did continue.)

Making a commitment implies the willingness to resort to force, and if the setting calls for it, large-scale force. Without a preponderance of deployable national power and the intent to use it, gestures intended to affirm commitments will fail. Thus a trip by the "Missouri," or indeed a whole task force, to Seoul in 1949 would not have averted the North Korean invasion (nor would a different text in Acheson's National Press Club speech) had the Russians and North Koreans felt that South Korean independence was not in fact a salient interest in American eyes. In a marginal case, as South Korea perhaps was, gestures could have been of use to signal intent, but only if they were congruent with policy (and domestic) attitudes—as perceived by others. In this respect, American willingness to accept the inevitable in China seemed to indicate a similar disposition with respect to Korea (provided that a Communist victory was made to seem equally inevitable); this was the "signal" that was perceived on the other side.

The inherent danger that supportive suasion may encourage the supported party to go too far has been discussed above and it was concluded that a restraining hand was often a necessary adjunct to the valiant arm. With respect to the active form of supportive suasion this same danger is easier to recognize.

In the 1958 Middle East crisis, Russian policy faced precisely this problem. To avoid an unwanted intensification of Egyptian activism, then already manifest in the attempt to subvert Lebanon and Jordan, Khrushchev reportedly told the Egyptians that the Russian effort to dissuade Anglo-American intervention against Revolutionary Iraq, and in the Levant, would not extend to the use of force on behalf of Egypt.[18] Once a Great Power acquires a client in a region, any attempt to apply deterrent coercion on other small powers in the area will evoke supportive effects upon the client, if both the Great Power and the client face the same adver-

[18] Muhamad Hasanain Haykal, *Al Ahram,* January 22, 1965.

35

saries. This is often a positive factor insofar as it strengthens the alliance relationship, but the client may also go too far from the senior partner's point of view; the client may try to exploit the patron in the expectation that forces will be made available to the client too, to protect it from imminent destruction.

By making it clear that his threats were strictly verbal, Khrushchev was trying to negate the supportive suasion inherent in his attempted exercise of coercive suasion against the United States and Britain. His warning that Russian help would not be forthcoming in the event of an Anglo-American attack on Egypt was calculated to dissuade "adventurism" in Cairo, and it was apparently reasonably successful. Had the Russians had a fleet on the scene, they could have tacitly achieved the same effect, but forcefully, by ordering Russian warships out of Egyptian ports and as far away as possible (so long as this move was not inconsistent with the attempt to deter Anglo-American intervention).

In 1950, elements of the U.S. Seventh Fleet were deployed between Taiwan and China proper to dissuade, and if need be, defeat any attempt at an amphibious invasion of Taiwan. At the same time, unintended supportive effects upon the Nationalists were neutralized by the public declaration that the Fleet would also intervene to prevent a Nationalist landing on the mainland. In this case, the deterrent effect on the Peking government was actually reinforced by the careful delimitation of the supportive role of the Seventh Fleet: its incentive to attempt an invasion of Taiwan was much reduced once the Nationalist threat to the mainland was neutralized, and a "virtuous circle" was thus set in train. Here again, the peculiar flexibility of naval forces enabled them to play a precisely defined role in a manner that has no equivalent on land.

In the context of the 1969–70 Egyptian-Israeli "War of Attrition," for example, when the Russians moved their antiaircraft missile regiments to Egypt to dissuade Israeli activism, they were automatically, and perhaps unintentionally, encouraging Egyptian activism. When the deployment was in place, complete with the rudiments of an integrated air defense system, fighter squadrons and the Goa batteries, the Russian forces were there for the Egyptian leadership to use, since these forces would have been forced to intervene in the event of a conflict, if only to defend themselves. And this was so whether they faced an Israeli air offensive (the move to be deterred) or a counter-offensive precipitated by an Egyptian artillery offensive, which the Russian deployment rendered more probable, whether the Russians wanted such an offensive or not.

As we have seen, the duality of effects produced by active suasion in a coercive mode presents a typical problem of alliance statecraft in the almost inevitable supportive effects thereby evoked. And the theoretically "defensive" nature of particular deployments is no insurance against their manipulation by junior partners. In the case of naval forces, moreover, the purported distinction between defensive and offensive forces lacks even a semblance of validity. At the same time, however, the flexibility of naval forces enables the deploying party to make precise mission distinctions. Moreover, should that not suffice, the senior partner can always order its fleet out of the area, thereby disabusing a client who wants to misuse a deployment meant only to deter others. And this can be done within a much shorter period of time and with none of the political costs or tactical dangers entailed by the withdrawal of land-based forces.

Since 1945, the U.S. Navy has exercised active suasion, support or coercive, deterrent or compellent, on more than seventy occasions [19] at all levels of intensity and upon areas of the globe ranging from the Caribbean to North Korea through Trieste. In each case the *sine qua non* for the successful evocation of the desired response has been the other side's perception of its warships, their tactical configuration and their intent. Chapter II is devoted to this essential aspect of naval suasion.

[19] A partial list, which stops short at 1969, and may otherwise be incomplete, is found in the addendum of a letter from Admiral T. H. Moorer to Senator Mondale, reproduced in U.S. Congress, *CVAN-70, Joint Hearings before the Senate and House Armed Services Committees,* 91st Cong., 2d Sess., 1970, pp. 163–65.

## II. VISIBILITY AND VIABILITY

In times of war, the misconceptions of peace, though not the intrusions of fortune, are filtered out in battle and the "true" balance of military power emerges, determining the outcome. But the *perceived* balance of forces that determines the outcome of "peacetime" confrontations can only be construed by men in terms of the predicted outcome of putative battle, and it is such predictions that determine political attitudes and, therefore, decisions. Each decision-maker must make his own assessment as best he can, in terms of whatever form of combat is envisaged, and he will often have to evaluate the other side's assessment, too. Unless actual fighting erupts, the interplay of potential military power in the conduct of relations between states is resolved only by the interaction of such predictions. It is therefore apparent that the *conditions* that govern the perception of military power are of overriding importance in evaluating its political applications.

First, it may safely be assumed that outside the strategic-nuclear arena, where quantitative evaluations are highly developed (though perhaps too esoteric to affect the perceptions of most political leaders), reasonable men will reject synthetic force-effectiveness comparisons based on elaborate, quantitative scenarios. Instead, the comparisons will begin with the salient capability data that may be available: gross tonnage levels, the number of ships by classes, aggregate gun and missile power, and so on. Other data, on equipment performance, for example, will often be channeled into the decision-making process in qualitative form: missiles will be said to be "deadly," very accurate, or indeed ineffectual; and guns will no doubt be described as "obsolete." Some equipment data of quite critical importance in actual combat may be overlooked or be altogether too intricate for consideration; therefore, sonar performance, missile reload capacity, and above all, electronic warfare capabilities will rarely be taken into account. The "dynamic" variables—seamanship, maintenance standards, and sensor/weapon skills under stress—will, of course, be recognized as important, but will often be discounted nevertheless since there is generally so little in the way of data to go by. At most, the "dynamic" variables of sea power will be subsumed under presumed national characteristics: an American warship will be rated higher than an Argentinian one, an Israeli ship higher than a Syrian, and so on. Not surprisingly, therefore, peacetime force comparisons can be grossly misleading indicators of true capabilities, and yet these are commonly the only variables that intrude upon the decisions that, in turn, determine the *political* effectiveness of naval forces.

From Versailles to Munich and beyond, the Italian Navy made Mussolini's Italy a great power in the Mediterranean. For two decades, in crises large and small, the Italian Navy, with its beautiful ships and poorly trained gun crews, more than earned its keep as it enabled Mussolini to have his way in Yugoslavia, Greece, Turkey, Spain, Ethiopia, and Albania. It was not only that the British did not want to fight, even in a war that they could win, but rather that they (like other observers) mistook form for substance.[20] Year after year, the Italian Navy budget was pre-empted by highly visible new ship acquisitions at the expense of such trifles as gunnery training, maintenance, and nonvisible (e.g., communications) equipment. The visible capabilities may have been spurious, but the political leverage that the Italian Navy secured for its master was all too real. It was not until 1940 that war provided the ultimate test of viability, exposing the basic weakness of the Italian Navy. Until then, even the British Admiralty had been deceived together with the Mediterranean powers, large and small, which chose to conciliate an Italy whose navy was as impressive as it was ineffectual.

The possibility of gross divergence between perceived capabilities, which determine political effectiveness, and combat viability has been substantially increased in recent years by the much greater significance of the "invisible" element in naval capabilities, primarily the quality of sensor and data-handling systems. One can always evaluate a four-gun "Skoryi" destroyer in Syrian hands as inferior to a one-gun U.S. Navy destroyer-escort by ignoring

[20] I am indebted to James E. King of the U.S. Naval War College for setting this issue in perspective. It was the unwillingness of the British to go to war at any price, even if they could win, that made the position of Mussolini so strong.

the nominal gun-power imbalance and resorting to high-confidence estimates of combat performance, based on recent experience in war. But how can one compare the ships of navies presumed to be competent which differ primarily in the quality of their "black boxes"? Little or nothing will be known about the precision and reliability of the hardware or about the expertise of the crews. Each side will know about his own black boxes, and electronic intelligence (and its variants) may tell a great deal about the other side, too. The Super Powers will thus be able to make some sort of estimate of each other's naval strength, but the smaller powers, which the Super Powers try to impress, coerce, or encourage with their navies, will not have this knowledge. Ordinarily, third-party leaders, whose perceptions determine their countries' policy-making, will form their views on the basis of the crudest sort of information, often qualitative, and primarily on the basis of what Russian and American media tell them.

In the light of the highly selective nature of political perceptions of naval power, one might be tempted to advocate ship configurations that emphasize explicitly the visible variables of naval power at the expense of those that are less transparent. Black boxes, whose classified performance plays no role in shaping third-party assessments of naval power, would accordingly be sacrificed in order to deploy more and bigger ships with more and bigger weapons. In the same vein, since missiles have more political "sex appeal" than guns, one would sacrifice the latter to get more of the former. It is instructive in this respect to compare in outline two hypothetical warships, one typically Russian and another American. At under six thousand tons of full-load displacement, the Russian ship would be described as a cruiser; its superstructure would reveal multiple (antiaircraft) guns, surface-to-surface missiles, antiaircraft missiles, and anti-submarine rocket-launchers. At around eight thousand tons, the American warship would be described as a destroyer, and its visible combat equipment would be limited to a single gun, a missile-launcher, and a helicopter. Nonexperts will see, and compare only what they see: the greater endurance, reload capability, and above all, the superior sensors of the American warship are likely to impinge much less than visible capabilities upon such nonexpert assessments.[21] If the comparison is made in terms of the rival fleets rather than single warships, as it should be, nonexpert assessments may be somewhat more perceptive of reality, in that the different (but of course

[21] The appearance of the "Kara" class cruisers, with their apparently greater endurance design-emphasis, may indicate a trend toward more capable but visually less impressive, warships, in the American style. On the other hand, the Chief of Naval Operations, in a Congressional communication has recently chosen to describe another new ship-class, the "Krivak" as the "most powerful warship ever built," ton per ton. Cited in Barry M. Blechman, *The Changing Soviet Navy* (Staff paper; Washington, D.C.: The Brookings Institution, 1973), p. 33.

congruent) mission-orientations would then emerge, thus improving evaluations (e.g., of the worth of sonar-heavy U.S. destroyer-escorts.)

Even so, perceptions are not only clouded by honest error but are also liable to be manipulated: during the 1930s, the Italian media did their best to promote a distorted view of the Mediterranean balance of power, and the distortion was most successful. Similarly, Russian media have persistently tried to equate the strength of the Russian Mediterranean squadron with that of the U.S. Sixth Fleet, though the once-confident assertions on the vulnerability of American carriers are no longer in evidence.[22]

In contrast to this, American media and official U.S. Navy statements relay a persistent message of decline in American naval power. This is evident, most recently, in the emphasis given to comparisons that stress the chronological age of American warships as compared to the Russian. Since these simplistic comparisons ignore both initial "maintainability" and the repeated modernization programs that virtually all major U.S. combatants have undergone, listings of Russian and American warships above and below some chronological line or other are, of course, entirely misleading.

More insidiously, Russian performance claims are taken at face value or indeed magnified, by

[22] This development may perhaps owe something to the fact that the first Russian angle-deck carriers are now reportedly undergoing sea trials.

44

focusing on hypothetical war scenarios calculated to enhance the relative strength of the Russian Navy, as in the "splendid" surprise attack scenario, where the U.S. Sixth Fleet becomes the victim of a coordinated ship-submarine and air-launched missile attack.

Whatever the imperatives of self-denigration imposed by the Congressional appropriations process, it is obvious that this official stance of the U.S. Navy must intrude on third-party perceptions of the (naval) balance of power. In the absence of full, or in many cases, any, technical knowledge, third-party political leaders will be influenced, as will public opinion, by what the media tell them. And while Russian media continue to relay maximal claims laced with old-fashioned bombast, American media will reflect only the Navy's cries of woe. The more sophisticated observers will discount the latter to some extent, mindful of the particular political circumstances that prevail in the United States, but even so, the message of American naval decline will nevertheless intrude on their perceptions. In this case, bad public relations function in a manner analogous to good advertising. America's friends and clients are discouraged and intimidated by the presumed adverse trend in the balance of naval power; her enemies, on the other hand, are encouraged to believe that they may harm American interests with impunity.[23]

[23] Altogether more important, though not germane to the argument, is the seepage of public relations attitudes into the

It has been argued above that both the configuration of the rival Super Power fleets and the impressionistic assessments conveyed by the media tend to produce the misleading impression of a Russo-American equipoise at sea, thus discounting the very wide margin of superiority conferred on the U.S. Navy by the carrier task forces, which applies to all combat settings but one, maximum-intensity conflict initiated by the Russian navy.

It is apparent that the higher the level of conflict-intensity envisaged in naval force-building, the greater will be the divergence between visible and actual capabilities, since more resources will be devoted to "invisibles," such as sophisticated sensor and data-handling systems. The resulting tendency to build warships with the highest technology content that is feasible minimizes the level of *perceived* capabilities, and to reiterate, these are the *only* capabilities that count in third-party evaluations of the strength of the rival fleets. While it would be the height of imprudence to make "political" missions which stop short of actual combat the

---

thought and disposition of the U.S. Navy. This is manifest in the defensive orientation of declared Navy strategy (and deployment policies), which remains inconsistent with the balance of forces at sea—in all but the "splendid" surprise attack context that only applies to a single fleet—and which is not consistent with the role of the (nonstrategic) Navy in the array of American military power as a whole. In the latter context, strategic nuclear forces and overseas land-based deployments are indeed defensive and reactive, and only the U.S. Navy can provide an offensive element in what would otherwise be an unbalanced defense-only posture.

*salient* mission—a process that would lead logically to the deployment of "cardboard" fleets on the interwar Italian model—it is evident that a mechanistic approach to force-planning, which demands maximum design sophistication in all components of the fleet, would minimize its politically useful "visible" power. In order to threaten—or support diplomatically—the littoral states, most of which are small powers, sophisticated sensors and advanced data systems would be redundant if combat should take place, and quite ineffectual if only *perceptions* are to be affected. It follows that one way of improving the political effectiveness of modern navies is to ensure that the level of presumed conflict intensity to which warships are designed is no higher than it must be, thus leaving more resources for less sophisticated but more visible power. To frighten South Yemen or encourage the Sheikh of Abu Dhabi one does not need a powerful sonar under the hull or a digital data system in the superstructure. If the saliency of political missions (and low-intensity conflict) is accorded the priority that the present state of international politics would seem to warrant (see Chapter III), force-planning may yet take the path of more visible and less sophisticated sea power.

In facing the visibility/viability dilemma, there is an important consolation: the "invisible" capabilities that only the deploying party sees are also useful in a political context, in that they enhance his own confidence. Since any political operation can degenerate into warfare, and since awareness of one's weaknesses intrudes on bargaining *conduct* (and position too, if word leaks out), the availability of capable "invisibles" can be a valuable insurance factor. Not only will resolve be strengthened, but it may also show through one's conduct, thus weakening the resolve of the adversary. But then, as in any form of insurance, there is a cost penalty for taking too much, as there is a risk penalty for taking too little.

It is likely that a better balance between visibility and viability will be struck in western navies when the new warship types now being built go into service. Whatever their intended tactical missions, warships such as the U.S. Sea Control Ship and Patrol Frigate, and the many types of missile-armed, fast patrol boats, all incorporate more in the way of visible capabilities and less in the way of "insurance" against the contingency of all-out combat with a sophisticated enemy—which can only be the Russian Navy. Since it seems that the Russian Navy is now moving toward a higher endurance (and more sophisticated) design pattern, we may see a convergence in future years between the two sides in this respect. (But the political utility of these new western warship types would be reduced if their weapon configurations mechanistically exclude all "visible power" requirements.)

The introduction of these new warship types could, in particular, restore the full (perceived offensive) potential of the carrier task forces, which remain the formidable centerpiece of American sea power. Sophisticated observers the world over have become aware of the fact that the Russian fleet (and naval air) now detracts considerably from the net offensive potential of the U.S. Navy. Though these observers may not have calculated the number of (defensive) "combat air patrol" sorties as opposed to those devoted to "projection," and though they may not be aware of the precise implications of the transition from the attack carrier concept to the new all-round carrier configuration, they must nevertheless presume that some such effect is at work, even if they have discounted the repeated—and authoritative—Russian statements according to which the U.S. Navy is now "neutralized" by its Russian counterpart. As for less sophisticated third-country leaders, it would take at least content-analysis and probably mind-reading for us to determine whether such technical factors intrude on their perceptions of the naval balance. One is inclined to think not. In the context of the 1970 Syria-Jordan crisis, for example, it is scarcely probable that the Syrian leaders assessed the threat posed by the U.S. Sixth Fleet in terms of, say, the number of strike sorties per day that its aircraft could deliver—as reduced by the number of defensive sorties needed to guard against a Russian attack.

More important, perhaps, is the long-term global trend in the relative offensive capabilities of Super Power navies *vis-à-vis* those of the air and naval forces of smaller powers. Until the early 1960s, the very wide *qualitative* gap between U.S. carrier air wings and the air power of countries such as Egypt, India, or Indonesia made any quantitative comparisons seem redundant. No small power thought of sustained *air* combat against U.S. Navy air wings as at all feasible, defensively or offensively. The Hawker-Hunters, Mig-17s, and Mystere IVs deployed by small power air forces (with a few Mig-19s and Super-Mysteres) and their pilots and ground facilities were seen—correctly—as grossly inferior to the fighter and attack squadrons on board U.S. carriers. Moreover, a pair of U.S. Navy carriers could contain a larger number of aircraft than was to be found in the first-line echelon of most small power air forces (in operational condition).

Since that time, the size of small power air forces in the Third World has increased very considerably. In the Mediterranean basin, for example, the number of combat [24] aircraft deployed by littoral states was estimated in 1973 at 620 for Egypt, 488 for Israel, and 326 for Syria as against 370, 260, and 94 respectively in 1965; [25] five years before that, only Egypt and Israel had any supersonic jet fighters—roughly one squadron per country. The most recent figures are inflated (since many aircraft are

---

[24] Jet fighters, combat-capable jet trainers, light bombers.

[25] *The Military Balance 1973–74* (London: The International Institute for Strategic Studies), pp. 31–36; and for the 1965 figures, J. L. Sutton and Geoffrey Kemp, *Arms to Developing Countries, 1945–65* (London: The Institute for Strategic Studies, 1966), p. 36.

not serviceable and pilots are in short supply) ; even so, it is apparent that the Sixth Fleet air wings have now become a "small" air force by local standards. In addition, the *net* perceived technical superiority of the Sixth Fleet's air wings has been eroded by the introduction of relatively advanced aircraft, such as late-model Mig-21 and Phantom II F-4 in small-power air forces.

Sober observers will not equate local air forces with the carrier air wings of the U.S. Navy on a one-for-one basis, but even when due allowances are made for qualitative differentials in crew skills, electronic support, and "ground" control, it is obvious that American naval air power has lost the net qualitative ascendancy that was the key to its political potency. The same trend will *a fortiori* affect the Russian carrier force now on the eve of deployment. Outfitted with twenty-five or so short take-off fighter class aircraft each, these Russian carriers will no doubt be useful for a wide variety of tactical missions but will not be able to make much of an impression in regions such as the eastern Mediterranean and the Indian subcontinent where local air forces are both large and sophisticated.

At the same time, increased utilization of the new class of missile-armed patrol boats has reduced the profile of the surface elements of Super Power fleets. So long as the locale of confrontations remains adjacent to the coastal waters of littoral states, small power navies equipped with missile boats will no longer be decisively outmatched by Super Power

CARL A. RUDISILL LIBRARY
LENOIR RHYNE COLLEGE

fleet elements, however superior in tonnage. The days when any one battleship could outmatch an entire small power navy have gone; the sea-based missile has emerged as the great equalizer.

But these detractions from the political utility of Super Power navies apply only when they are intended to affect the outcome of local confrontations. This has not affected the symbolic role of Super Power fleets. Where naval forces are introduced in order to affirm the commitment of national power in all its dimensions, their actual tactical capabilities do not delimit their political effectiveness. Thus, for example, the undoubted ability of Israeli air and naval forces to dispose of any Russian naval forces in the eastern Mediterranean in short order does not nullify their utility as instruments of armed suasion. It is the over-all political context that will determine the political effectiveness of Super Power navies, and not their tactical capabilities, since it is this context that governs the application of national power, the true determinant, of which the naval element is only one constituent.

# III. THE POLITICAL CONTEXT

In World Wars I and II, which remain the classical models of the exercise of force in the minds of many, political considerations scarcely seemed to intrude upon the conduct of hostilities. But since 1945, as most often before 1914, war has once again been subjected to the discipline of political purpose, which imposes many constraints on the use of force. Once tactical gains are compared to political costs, each side sets its own limitations on the use of its own forces, so that war becomes "limited." The modern concept of Limited War is not modern at all but rather analogous to most pre-1914 European wars.

This century's experience of apolitical total war has taught us two lessons which are now generally (but not universally) accepted; first, that it is only a continuous re-evaluation of the political goals pursued which can make warfare a rational activity, in the formal sense of ends-means alignment; and second, that if the political dimension of war is not accorded an overriding priority, the use of force will often be ineffectual, and may even be perverted to the advantage of the very enemy against whom force was applied in the first place. In this respect, the errors of *all* sides in the Indochina war, too well known to bear repetition, provide an infinity of examples of the misapplication of force.

It is apparent that these lessons also apply to the exercise of armed suasion, only more so, since armed suasion in all its forms always remains at the lower end of the intensity spectrum and can never reach the spasm of "total" war leading to unconditional surrender or societal destruction. The dominating framework of armed suasion is thus the domestic, international, and local (i.e., target-country) political context, which in combination will determine the absolute feasibility, and degree of success, of its exercise.

## THE DOMESTIC ENVIRONMENT

The *domestic* setting is clearly the key parameter of any exercise of armed suasion on the part of the western powers. Within the limits afforded by the authority, prerogatives, and manipulative skills of their chief executives, the ability of these powers to exercise naval suasion will be determined by others' perceptions of relevant domestic opinion and its parliamentary representation. At this particular time, for example, it is apparent to most observers that the American public's willingness to use force on behalf of allies and clients is exceedingly limited; American "national interests" have been redefined, and much more narrowly than before. Especially in the American case, however, domestic attitudes are volatile and apt to undergo sudden changes. No more will be said on this score, except to remark that the over-all effect of this particular mood is a sharp reduction in the suasion potential of American military power. The primarily *local* political determinants will be analyzed below in a series of illustrative examples.

54

## *Unilateral Suasion: The Russo-Finnish Case*

The gross imbalance in military power between the Soviet Union and Finland codified in the 1947 peace treaty (which limits the scale of Finnish armaments and denies an alliance option) has consistently yielded a very large degree of leverage over Finnish conduct to the Russian leadership. From the choice of successive Finnish presidents to the conduct of Finnish diplomacy, Russian influence and Russian control have been pervasive.[26] The small size of the country's population and economic base and its most unfavorable military geography have set a very low ceiling on Finland's defensive potential *vis-à-vis* the Soviet Union. Finland's

[26] With the popularization of the unfortunate term "Finlandization," the nature of Finno-Soviet relations has suddenly become a matter of debate among foreign policy experts. To justify the term "pervasive" in the above, the following established facts appear to be sufficient: (1) Finland has been barred from joining the EEC, even as a nonpolitical "associate" member, by a public "cease and desist" order issued in Moscow; (2) as noted above, the Russians retain a (public) veto right on the choice of Finnish presidents; and (3) the Finnish stance in international fora such as the UN (and now in the CES) is aligned with that of Moscow, with at most the right of abstention. The Russians have also exercised leverage on nongovernmental Finnish institutions through the influence of the Finnish presidential office (e.g., to coerce the Finnish Union of Students to host the 1962 IUS Festival and, most recently, to prevent a Helsinki publisher from printing the translated works of Russian dissenters, including a recent Nobel prize winner). From the trivial to that which intrudes in the daily economic life of the Finns, the Russians have frequently interfered in domestic matters, as in Finnish foreign policy, by using the "consultation" provisions of the 1947 peace treaty.

successive coalition governments, though dominated by anticommunist parties and dependent on a sometimes violently anti-Russian public opinion, have responded realistically to the latent (and sometimes active) suasion of Russian military power: whenever Moscow's desiderata have been made known, the Finns have complied with them.

With no shot fired since September 1944, and with none of the adverse effects on western opinion that would result from any use of actual force on their part, the Russians have thus continuously enjoyed substantial political returns from their net military superiority over Finland, and they do so still, regardless of the détente. The *international* setting that has rendered possible this most successful exercise of armed suasion is complicated; it includes Swedish neutrality, Finland's wartime antecedents, and the resultant ambiguity in Finland's status in the formative 1945–48 period.

But it is a *local* political phenomenon that appears to be salient: the "realistic" attitude of Finnish political elites and opinion at large. If the Finns were suddenly to become more bellicose or otherwise "unrealistic," the Russians would be faced with a grim choice: either to accept a loss of control over Finnish conduct or else impose it by direct force. If they opted for the former, they would face the supposed dangers resulting from Finnish adhesion to the West—dangers that men in the Kremlin are apt to rate much higher than external observers would. If they opted for the use of force, an invasion of Finland would be liable to drive Sweden into the nuclear option, dispel the atmospherics of the détente, shore up NATO, and so on.

It is apparent from the above that the fundamental *sine qua non* of the exercise of armed suasion is the "cooperation" of its targets. The political leaders of the target country must accept the intrusion and act as mediators between outside compulsion and their own public, thus manifesting the required suasion and validating the political worth of military power. The leaders must also persuade, or force, any relevant public to accept its own subordination to outside coercion. If either the political leaders or the relevant public of the target country do not accept the compulsion of necessity and choose to defy the threat, armed suasion in its coercive mode will fail, *regardless of the balance of forces between the two sides*. Thus, coercive suasion requires not only the other sides' recognition of the threat and his own inability to negate it, but also the *acceptance* of compliance as an imposed necessity. One need not follow from the other: It was for this very reason that the Russian attempt to exercise suasion over Czechoslovakia in 1968 failed.

## Noncooperation of the Public: Czechoslovakia 1968

Faced with Czech liberalization in the spring of 1968 (which some area experts believe posed an *internal* threat to the Soviet Union), the Russian leadership attempted to control the Prague government by means of active suasion in a decidedly coercive form, and in a predominantly compellent mode. Fully aware of the immense superiority of Russian military power, and knowing that they could count on no help from the West, the Czech leaders were nevertheless unable to comply with Russian demands. Czech opinion, now surfacing because of the very liberalization that the Russians wanted to curtail, refused to concede Russian military superiority its political due; this was enough to nullify Russian coercive suasion. Only the cooperation of the Czechs could have converted Russian military power into effective political leverage, and since this vital ingredient was missing, the Russians were forced to *use* their military power. The decision to invade implied the acceptance of serious political costs and potentially grave risks, though in the event both were of course minimized by the failure of the Czech leaders to manifest the will to fight, and by an awareness of the passivity of western opinion, which minimized the external repercussions of the invasion. One way of defeating coercive suasion is, of course, to reduce its net benefits to the would-be "compellor" by raising the costs, and risks, of the threat operation, as in the case described below.

## Successful Counter-Suasion: Romania and Yugoslavia, 1968

The Russian incentive to use force against the "nationalist-deviationists" in Belgrade and Bucharest was much smaller to begin with than in the Czech case. The Czech liberalization was raising the political temperature in the Ukraine, and it was this *internal* threat that experts declare to be the salient motive of the Kremlin's hostility to the "Prague Spring."

Nevertheless, it is apparent that the threat of a Russian invasion was taken seriously in both Romania and Yugoslavia, and the response was a classic instance of counter-suasion.[27] When, in the aftermath of the invasion of Czechoslovakia, Tito reportedly told the Russian ambassador that there was a bullet waiting for every Russian that dared to cross the frontier, the anachronism of his imagery did nothing to detract from the effectiveness of Yugoslav counter-suasion. At the same time, the Romanian leaders publicly proclaimed their readiness to fight, and attempted to improvise the rudiments of an armed militia. In both cases, the *net* incentive to the Russians of an invasion was reduced by the threat of guerrilla warfare against any invaders.

It may be doubted whether the Russians in fact contemplated an invasion of the two countries in 1968, but it is certain that without successful counter-suasion, the Kremlin would have been able to enjoy the same ascendancy over Belgrade's policy

[27] Counter-suasion as here used is not meant as a new, separate concept—more than enough have been introduced already. The term merely describes the bilateral exercise of suasion, whose possibility was implicit throughout the discussion, and which raises no new analytical problems.

that it enjoys over Helsinki's. In the Romanian case, on the other hand, the degree of independence accorded to Romanian foreign policy would certainly have been curtailed.

## Counter-Suasion and Deflection: The Russo-Turkish Case

The cases examined so far have all been zero-sum situations where what one party concedes the other gains, and vice versa. This example is typical of the interaction of alliance and external relations, and the gains and losses are no longer fully reciprocal.

No longer presenting a direct threat to the integrity of Turkish national territory, and no longer demanding formal revision of the Straits navigation regime, the Soviet Union has nevertheless successfully exercised armed suasion over Turkey, even while maintaining a fairly benevolent stance, which includes significant aid flows. Faced with a sharp relative increase in Russian strategic and naval power, and eager to normalize relations with their formidable neighbor, the Turks have chosen to conciliate the Russians, and have been able to do so at little or no direct cost to themselves. It is only in respect to strategic transit that Turkey is of primary importance to the Soviet Union, and this is the area where the concessions have been made. Examples of such deflection, where the Russians are conciliated at the expense of western rather than specifically Turkish interests, include the overland traffic agreement (unimpeded Russian transit to Iraq and Syria by road), the generous Turkish interpretation of the Montreux Convention, which regulates ship movements in the Straits, and above all, the overflight permissions accorded to Russian civilian and military aircraft across Turkish airspace.

The alliance relationship in NATO and with the United States no doubt retains a measure of validity in Turkish eyes, but it is apparent that its supportive effect is not enough to counteract Russian suasion, especially since the coercion is latent and packaged in a benevolent, diplomatic stance.

## THE INTERNATIONAL ENVIRONMENT

The fashionable concept of the hour, "multipolarity," is a legitimate description of what was until recently a salient goal of American foreign policy, i.e., the assumption of power by new centers, Europe, China, and Japan, all of which are bound to be in greater opposition to Moscow than to Washington. It is obvious that the United States could maintain the equilibrium of the international system at a lower price in blood and treasure if new power centers emerged and took over part of the burden. (The implicit assumption is that, for organic reasons, the supposed new centers will absorb and deflect Russian, and not American, power.) But if multipolarity describes an American systemic goal, it certainly does not describe the current international system. For *economic* polycentrism cannot be converted into (political) multipolarity unless either the new "poles" acquire a *military* dimension to their power *or,* alternatively, the dé-tente results in a situation where military power is no longer a useful component of national power.

Neither of these two conditions has been ful-filled. There is no need to go into the details of force-level statistics to prove that the two Super Powers retain an overwhelming superiority in in every dimension of military power which fully justifies their title. As for a decline in the importance of military power in the conduct of international relations, the examples given above as well as the very fact that a Conference on European Security is taking place, that the Mutual Force Reduction talks are deemed significant, and that nations around the world daily accord the Russians a status that neither their antiquated economy, dormant culture, nor obsolete ideological claims would warrant, prove beyond all possible doubt that there is no such de-cline. What is true, of course, is that the *western* propensity to use force has declined, but this hardly proves the point.

However, one aspect of the multipolar concept does describe a real, ongoing phenomenon: the level of independence of the small powers has in-deed been increasing, though the ultimate cause of this trend is more their reduced significance to the Super Powers (owing to the "waning of ideology") than the supposed rise of new power centers that neutralize each other.

The politics of the Mediterranean region at the

present time illustrate the trend very well: American influence over the region has declined considerably since the 1950s,[28] and the Soviet Union, once regarded by many as the irresistible "wave of the future," has lost much of its short-lived influence. With their presence so firmly implanted in Egypt, the Russians were supposedly about to extend their base infrastructure all the way to Algeria, or so it seemed only a few years ago. Today, the Soviet Union's active military presence is limited to the easternmost corner of the Arab world, where its survival is contingent on the goodwill of the Iraqi regime of the day. Does this portent of multipolarity (i.e., small power independence) imply in itself a reduction in the political utility of Super Power naval forces? Since there has been an undoubted loss of influence on the part of the Super Powers, an affirmative answer may appear logical. In fact, such a conclusion is likely to be premature.

Consider the opposite case, the "bipolarity" that was. Describing a world in which every state was supposedly under the influence, control, or protection—or at least aligned with—one or the other of the Super Powers, "bipolarity" restricted to a great extent the opportunities for the exercise of armed suasion. As soon as a Super Power attempted to

[28] The recent (1974) activism of American diplomacy in the wake of the October 1973 war does not entail a genuine restoration of American influence unless in a most superficial sense. Amicable relations between Cairo and Washington do not mean that Egypt will comply with American *desiderata*.

evoke coercive suasion effects from a small power, the other Super Power was liable to rush to the scene in order to counter and, if possible, negate such suasion. In a perfect bipolar world, for example, the American attempt to compel the Syrians to withdraw from Jordan in 1970 would have induced a contrary move on the part of the Russians, so that American coercive suasion would have been absorbed or even negated by Russian supportive suasion. In fact, any exercise of coercive suasion by a Super Power would have entailed the risk of a central confrontation with the other Super Power, even if the locale was remote and the interests in dispute quite marginal.

In the early 1960s, when international reality approached the abstraction of bipolarity, Russians and Americans were willing to take major risks over Cuba, the Congo, and Laos. In those balmy days every State Department desk officer could hope to interest the highest officials of the land in the politics of Burundi or the danger of communist penetration in the fifty-man trade union federation of Rwanda. Similarly, those countries that turned toward Moscow found that a couple of anti-American speeches sufficed to obtain Russian applause, a gift of a shipload of tractors, generous supplies of weapons, and a Lenin prize for the ruling potentate. Today things are very different. Even a country with the considerable regional status and economic importance of Chile can twice cross over the former bipolar lines without precipitating an intervention by

the "losing" Super Power or stimulating much en-
thusiasm on the part of the "winner."

As a general principle, it may be asserted that in
a world which is decreasingly bipolar (though not
truly multipolar either) the scope for armed suasion is greater, and the risks smaller, since the likeli-
hood of counter-suasion by the other Super Power is
also much smaller. This results from the fact that
small power links with one or the other of the Super
Powers involve a decreasing degree of control and
protection, and the number that can still count on
the automatic support of the Super Powers is stead-
ily shrinking.

### THE REGIONAL ENVIRONMENT: THE MEDITERRANEAN EXAMPLE

Translating these abstractions into the current
Mediterranean political scene, it is apparent that
reality does bear some resemblance to theory.

Only in the case of four of the fifteen kingdoms,
regencies, and republics of the Mediterranean basin
are there processes of government that may be
deemed to be representative. Nevertheless, in the
case of many of these countries, the "cooperation"
of the public (or at least the *urban* public), and not
only that of the ruling group, is required in order
to validate any major exercise of armed suasion.
There may be no legislature and no elective process,
but the "street" remains a powerful factor, especially in Arab politics, and it can vote by riot and
mob action even if denied the ballot. Since the

"street" is generally poorly informed about the international realities that dominate small power conduct, and since it normally reflects an extreme nationalism (in form if not always in content), obstacles to, and distortions of, all forms of armed suasion are likely to result. As the Israelis have repeatedly discovered (and they have had to re-learn the lesson time after time), the ability to pose a threat to valuable Arab targets is no guarantee that street opinion will allow leaders in Beirut or Damascus to respond "realistically" to the threat.

Similarily, Russian attempts at *supportive* suasion, through, say, the rotation of ships in Egyptian ports vulnerable to attack, may be stripped of much of their significance since Egyptian opinion would not readily *recognize* the import of the move and is therefore liable to protest against Russian "inaction" on behalf of Egypt. Likewise, it is obvious that an ill-informed and potentially explosive public opinion will impede the exercise of American naval suasion in the prospective target countries, by raising its costs and introducing risks. The governing elites themselves may be fully aware of their weakness, but compliance with outside demands may well be seen as evidence of timidity (or personal subornation) by a public whose view of the world and of the forces within it may bear only a distant resemblance to reality as seen by others. The fact that the governing elites themselves promoted such distortions of reality does not alter their constraining effect: they may well remain prisoners of the visions they themselves have created. In this respect, the use of *symbolic* force may come into its own; it may help the rulers to persuade the ruled of the necessity of compliance, by giving a tangible quality to the threat.

That genuine multipolarity is not with us as yet is quite obvious in the Mediterranean context. When President Anwar Sadat sent his envoys to Europe and China in the aftermath of the 1972 Russian expulsion/withdrawal, they discovered that both the road to peace (through a settlement imposed on Israel) and to war (through much increased Chinese military aid) would still have to go through Washington or Moscow. Self-important as officials in London, Paris, or Peking may be, they were still unable to deliver the goods: these new polar centers are simply not up to the task. Paris may sell a few (expensive) aircraft; London, too, can do this; and Peking looms large to the guerrillas whose simple weapons come from China. But the undoubted weakening of the position and activism of the Super Powers cannot make polar centers out of what are—at most—only *economic* powers.

On the other hand, the Super Powers' unbenevolent neglect has undoubtedly given a greater freedom of action to the small powers of the Third World, while leaving them more exposed than ever to outside coercion. Israel is certainly more vulnerable to Russian coercion [29] than it once was. Libya may have friends in Paris but they could not, and

[29] The unpublicized but highly effective Russian nuclear threat of October 1973 is only the most recent and spectacular example.

would not, protect her if others should choose to treat her as the Barbary states were once treated. Albania is now open to Russian naval suasion if any value was to be found in it. Even Turkey can no longer rely on the exclusive protection of the Alliance and sees virtue in conciliating Russian interests instead of negating them, as she did in the pristine years of the Cold War. After longing for greater independence for so long, the small powers of the Third World may soon come to the conclusion that dependence had its virtues after all.

But the freedom and solitude of this multipolarity-without-new-poles is a fragile phenomenon. Since the Super Powers retain their overwhelming military superiority over all others, the pattern of bipolarity is apt to re-emerge at any time, and in full force, as a result of external shocks or internal developments that may be sudden and obscure. This is of limited significance to the small powers but quite critical for the Super Powers: if either reverts to a more forceful policy, it may induce a collapse of the détente-cum-multipolarity, and they may find themselves in an old-style bipolar confrontation.

This introduces a new element of uncertainty into the exercise of armed suasion. If either Super Power were to exploit the opportunity offered by depolarization to apply coercive pressures on the small powers of the Third World, it may discover that this would suffice to destroy the very setting that made the move possible in the first place.

In many ways, the risks of the former bipolar

world, with its clear lines of demarcation, were both less insidious and more manageable, since a direct confrontation in the old style was at least simpler to control than the systemic disruption that may now result if the Super Powers act to defend their interests. And this is the crux of the problem: the present noninterventionist attitude would be stable if these interests had been abandoned, but they have not been, and cannot be, simply abandoned.[30]

[30] The retention of all major interests (i.e., commitments), without commensurate investments in blood or treasure for their defense, is one way of describing the Nixon doctrine. In practice, however, both Super Powers have abandoned their most marginal interests. But this may reflect localized responses to local problems of peculiar intractability.

# IV. TACTICS

It is characteristic of the confusion that prevails with respect to the political application of naval power in the context of suasion, as opposed to combat, that the "tactical" inputs are often treated as if they were outputs. In a combat context, we speak of the outputs, such as projection capabilities (in terms of the number of sorties) and gunfire support (in terms of the weight of salvo), and not of the inputs, i.e., the deployment of $X$ aircraft or $Y$ guns. Similarly, in a suasion context, "flag-showing (missions)" and "interposition" are only inputs; the outputs are the various forms and modes of naval suasion, i.e., the reactions of others that are in fact evoked. Since we have discussed only the outputs of suasion in the above, the table that follows is intended to provide a *tentative* listing and classification of the "tactical" inputs of naval suasion, alongside some mention of the suasion effects that they are meant to evoke. All the inputs are associated with the exercise of active suasion, since latent suasion is of course undirected.

Many more tactical variations have no doubt been recorded in the long history of naval suasion.[31]

[31] The Athenians have in particular left us a detailed record of their imaginative exercise of naval suasion. The trireme fleet was kept in service in "peacetime" from the time of Themistocles to the beginning of the Peloponnesian War; its commanders were political appointees rather than specialists; and the political dimension of naval power was well understood. In particular, it was realized that the size of the fleet (200 boats) reflected the level of Alliance resources and the scope of

Though the list in Table II is hardly likely to be exhaustive, it does suggest the wide range of possible inputs that a fleet may generate in order to evoke the desired type of suasion. It also suggests the wisdom of introducing the "tactical" requirements of naval suasion as a subject of naval training and fleet exercises in an explicit manner so as to fill the gaps left by combat-oriented "tactics," which are not always identical with those most suitable for political purposes. In particular, the reconnaissance capabilities of the target states, adversaries, third parties, or clients may be inadequate to allow the required perception of the "tactics" listed above, unless the latter are designed explicitly to facilitate such observation. In addition, of course, there will be diplomatic and media communications, but these will not normally be a naval responsibility as such. In general, it may be true that navies are more attentive than land-based forces to the political dimension of military power, but a prolonged concentration on combat operations would certainly erode this awareness. In any case, a greater emphasis on the "tactics" of naval suasion is warranted at this time by the official reformulations of

---

Athenian ambitions, rather than a response to the scale of perceived enemy threats. Athenians would not have thought it wise to reduce the size of their fleet merely because the Persian/Phoenician or Corinthian threat waned. Their deployment strategy was not responsive, but rather intended to provide the means needed for a positive affirmation of Athenian political goals. When war came, however, this "political" fleet fought, and by all accounts, it fought well.

both Russian and American naval strategy that the present phase of détente has inspired.[32]

[32] See in this connection the ever-greater emphasis given to the political side of things in successive Navy (CNO) posture statements, and especially compare FY 1974 (forthcoming) with, say, FY 1966. For the reformulation of Russian naval strategy, see Clyde A. Smith, "The Meaning and Significance of the Gorhkov Articles," *Naval War College Review,* March–April 1974, pp. 18–37. Translations of the eleven Gorhkov articles are being published in the *United States Naval Institute Proceedings* on a monthly basis, January–November 1974.

*For Table II see page 74*

TABLE II. THE INPUTS OF NAVAL SUASION

## A. Force-Level Changes

| | |
|---|---|
| a. Reinforcements: | 1. To augment the intensity of coercive or supportive suasion. |
| | 2. To "show concern" where no specific goals obtain. |
| | 3. To pre-empt Super Power suasion that a local client may invoke against the deploying party or *his* client; and variants of.[a] |
| b. Reductions: | 1. To signal disengagement. |
| | 2. To discourage, specifically, the unwanted activism of a local client. |

[a] In an unpublished paper on naval strategy in the Mediterranean, James E. King has developed the concept of "pre-emptive intervention," which is to hold the middle ground between deterrence (which is anticipatory) and compellence (which operates *ex post facto*). The concept is particularly useful to describe "triangular" exercises of suasion whose targets are both a local power and its patron (whose intervention is to be prevented).

|  | 3. To close combat options in order to facilitate resistance to pressures for their use on own or client's behalf, including domestic pressures. |
|---|---|

### B. Display Manipulations

| a. Fleet movements and maneuvers in adversary's and/or client's presumed zone of observation: | 1. To evoke coercive or supportive effects in general where no direct relationship to any enemy threats obtains. |
|---|---|
|  | 2. To show concern in general where no specific goals or client affiliations obtain, i.e., in a crisis involving only third parties, or only allies. |
| b. Port visits and transits in direct proximity to land: | 1. Same as effects 1 and 2, directly above. More suitable for effects on public opinion as opposed to the ruling groups only. Essentially supportive but not always, i.e., in passage through Suez Canal or Dardanelles. |

| | |
|---|---|
| c. Display of combat capabilities in action where no direct relationship to any specific threat obtains: | 1. To augment intensity of effects 1 and 2 in B/a, above. |
| d. Display of *specific* combat capabilities in action where these are appropriate to counter a specific enemy threat or to pose an equally specific threat (e.g., ASW display if enemy submarine threat to friendly shipping; amphibious display to threaten a landing, etc.) : | 1. To augment intensity of effects 1 and 2 in B/a, above. 2. To render coercion and/or support, narrow and limited as opposed to general and open-ended. Where the aim is to avoid a stance of general opposition (or support) and to convey intention to oppose some specific enemy acts, or require a specific act of compliance, or support a client in some particular respect, and not in any venture he may be contemplating. |

C. Fleet Configuration Changes

| | |
|---|---|
| a. Increase/reduction in battle readiness (i.e., withdrawal of logistic support | 1. To augment/reduce intensity of coercive or supportive effects in general. |

ships and any noncombatant auxiliaries; or on the contrary, anticipation of routine replenishment or maintenance operations, etc.) :

2. To signal concern/disengagement in general.

b. Task-force selection out of normally deployed fleet to accentuate specific combat capabilities:

1. To augment suasion effects, as above, further.

2. To limit scope of coercion or support to a narrower range of own-side actions (e.g., to deter, say, a Syrian attack on Lebanon, or compel a withdrawal, task force sent—as per A and B—but without amphibious elements in order to prevent others' perception of own-side intention to land or occupy).

D. Warship Configuration Changes

a. Increase/reduction of battle readiness in crew dispositions, signaling procedures, etc.:

1. Effects same as 1 and 2 in C/a, above.)

| | |
|---|---|
| b. Where applicable, *specific* type of battle readiness (e.g., carrier aircraft sent up for CAP and ASW only; or for attack too; gunfire readiness or ASW readiness only). Applicable where ship flexibility obtains, and where data available to prospective targets of suasion: | 1. Effects same as 1 and 2 in C/b, above. |

E. Use of Capabilities

| | |
|---|---|
| a. Intrusive reconnaissance by naval aircraft or ships in direct proximity to land or adversary warships: | 1. To deter adversary moves by signaling advance knowledge and possibility of alerting the prospective targets. |
| | 2. To intensify coercive or supportive effects in general in association with other moves under A,B,C,D. |
| | 3. To suggest preparation for particular combat actions (e.g., air strikes) |

|  | in association with B/d, C/b, or D/b. |
|---|---|
| b. Interposition of fleet units between third-party or adversary warships and their targets; to provide close escort of threatened shipping; to "intercept" amphibious landings, etc.: | 1. To *reinforce* deterrence or compellence, or provide support to clients. <br><br> 2. To render suasion effects specific, and therefore limit the scope of intervention in others' eyes, as per B/d. |
| c. "Symbolic" and nondestructive force, e.g., forcing D/E submarines to the surface by continuous pursuit; harassment of adversary ship movements (other than interposition); deliberate off-target shooting or air attack; infliction of minor damage seen to have been deliberately minimized, etc.: | 1. Effects same as 1 and 2 in E/b. |

*Note: All* of the above (A–E) to be coupled if required with diplomatic/media "signaling."

**Library of Congress Cataloging in Publication Data**

Luttwak, Edward N
  The political uses of sea power.

  (Studies in international affairs, no. 23)
  Includes bibliographical references.
  1. Sea-power. 2. World politics. I. Title.
II. Series: Washington Center of Foreign Policy
Research. Studies in international affairs, no. 23.
V25.L86      359.03'0904      74–8219
ISBN 0–8018–1658–0
ISBN 0–8018–1659–9 (pbk.)